90 days of inspiration

TAMURA J. GADSON

Not Really Random Ltd. Co.

Copyright © 2021 Tamura J. Gadson

All rights reserved. No part of this publication may be reproduced, stored or transmitted in any form or by any means, electronic, mechanical, photocopying, recording, scanning, or otherwise without written permission from the publisher. It is illegal to copy this book, post it to a website, or distribute it by any other means without permission.

Designations used by companies to distinguish their products are often claimed as trademarks. All brand names and product names used in this book and on its cover are trade names, service marks, trademarks and registered trademarks of their respective owners. The publishers and the book are not associated with any product or vendor mentioned in this book. None of the companies referenced within the book have endorsed the book.

Scripture quotations are taken from the Holy Bible, New Living Translation, copyright © 1996, 2004, 2015 by Tyndale House Foundation. Used by permission of Tyndale House Publishers, Carol Stream, Illinois 60188. All rights reserved.

ISBN: 978-1-7354595-0-9

Published by
Not Really Random Ltd. Co.
P.O. Box 603
Suwanee GA 30024
www.notreallyrandom.com

Cover Art: Shahbail Shabbir

Welcome, my fellow traveler. I dedicate this book to you. It is my honor and privilege to be your guide on your journey to self-discovery, self-acceptance, and self-love.

The book was designed purposely to be read and used how you, the traveler on this journey, deem fit. After each thought, you will find the space to journal and reflect on what you have read. Along this journey, you may experience a wide range of emotions. Allow yourself to feel them all.

My fellow traveler, if I can leave one thing with you as you begin your journey, please remember no matter how old you are or where you are in your life's journey, there is always joy to be found.

Happy travels.

Table Of Contents

Move Your Feet	1
Need a Boost	3
Run Your Race	5
Lemons of Life	7
Who's There?	9
Organization of Me	11
Seasons	13
Enough	15
Happy Yet?	17
Change of Focus	19
Purposefully Designed	21
Attention Please	23
Thirsty	25
Perfect Practice	27
Bend Not Break	29
Is This Me?	31
Will You Go?	33
Freedom	35
Don't Think, Know	37
Lost and Found	39
Remove the Plastic	41
Time for Cake	43
In the Middle	45
Run	47
Ugly Mess	49
Go Get it	51
Simon Says	53
Vision	55
Mad for What?	57
Left for Dead	59
Handle Your Truth	61
Little Red Hen	63
Burned Bridge?	65
Beautiful Reflection	67
Love	69
Friends	71
What You Eat	73
Heart's Desire	75
Sister's Keeper	77
Stop Thief	79
Step Out	81
Yes and No	83
Fat Lady, Who?	85
Comfort	87
No More Tears	89
Clap Your Hands	91
Inside Voice	93
You vs. You	95
Elephant	97
Stay	99
Truth or Dare	101
Sacrifice	103
Restoration	105
Direction	107
Bear the wait	109
Overflow	111
Not Broken	113
Remember	115
Faith over Fear	117
Silence	119
Break Habits	121
Love's Foundation	123
Hold This	125
Labor of Love	127
Beautiful Creations	129
Posture Correction	131
Your Story	133
All Aboard	135
Narrative	137
Are You Blind?	139
What's Missing?	141
Whole	143
Helping Hand	145
Speak Out	147
Broken Blessings	149
Thrive	151
Hold On	153
Amendments	155
The Present	157
Sanctuary	159
By Invitation Only	161
Listen	163
Weakest Link?	165
Taste Buds	167
Own It	169
Mine	171
Clean Up	173
Life Lesson	175
Faith's Escape	177
Sunflowers	179

Move Your Feet

When my daughter first become interested in learning how to drive, she asked if I would teach her. So, being the wonderful mother that I am, I took her driving. While we sat in the empty parking lot, she asked me the purpose of each pedal. I explained one was the gas, and the other was the brake. She responded with okay, then she started the car and proceeded to place one foot on the gas and the other on the brake. I let out the loudest scream of no, which scared her and frustrated me.

At that moment I asked myself how often do we go through life with one foot on the gas and the other on the brake? How often do we go through life with both feet on both pedals at the same time?

That is the question for today. Do you have your foot on the brake and the gas pedal of life? Do you play it safe when making decisions?

Here is the challenge for today. Pick one. Oh, there will be times when you will need to overcome fears and frustration, and move full speed ahead. Other moments will cause you to proceed with caution and brake a moment's notice. Know that neither is good or bad, but think about this. If you have one foot on the brake and one foot on the gas, the possibilities of your moving forward are very slim.

For any movement to gain momentum, it must start with a small action.

• *Adam Braum*

Need a Boost

I am not a very tall woman. In fact, I often need assistance to reach items on the top shelves. On one particular day, I felt a bit vertically challenged while putting up groceries. I was trying to reach the cabinet above the refrigerator. I asked my daughter to grab the step stool for me. While I stood on the step stool, this thought came to mind.

Here is the question for today. Have you ever experienced a step stool moment, a situation designed to elevate you higher?

Here is the challenge for today. Recognize when situations, experiences, chance encounters, or meetings are designed to help you reach your next goal, your next level of purpose. Not all jobs, relationships, or friendships are intended for permanence. Now, understand I am not saying to step on or manipulate people or situations to get where you want to go. Use the lessons, assistance, or mentoring opportunities to help step you further into your purpose.

*Those who are happiest are those who do
the most for others.*

· Booker T. Washington

Run Your Race

When I decided to begin my journey toward a healthier lifestyle, I thought taking up running or speed walking would be a great thing to do. What I did not expect was my that competitive nature would take over. I became frustrated and upset when "seasoned" or mature individuals passed me.

One day when I was talking with a friend about my experience and frustrations, she said, "Joy, you're not in competition with anyone else but yourself. This is your race your pace."

I left our conversation renewed and with a sense of purpose. The next time I was out running and a seasoned individual passed me, instead of getting upset, I began to repeat to myself the mantra of "My race, my pace."

Here is the question for today. To whom are you comparing yourself? With whom are you competing?

The challenge for today is to know that your life moves at your pace. No need to be envious, jealous, or discouraged at what someone else may have. Your race, your pace. You have unique gifts and talents to help you run your race. In the end, it does not matter how you look while running your race. You just need to start moving. In the words of a Nike advertisement, "Just do it."

So I run straight to the goal with purpose in every step.

• *1 Corinthians 9:26* •

Lemons of Life

"When life gives you lemons, make lemonade." How many times have we heard that said when a person has fallen on hard or difficult times? It is generally intended to provide the person with cheer or comfort.

The statement should not be when life gives you lemons, make lemonade. Instead, it should be, "How you handle the lemons life hands to you is up to you."

Here is the question for today. When presented with the lemon, did you instantly bite into it, tasting the bitterness and sourness of it? Or did you let it sit for a moment, allowing the taste to permeate your senses? Did you allow yourself the opportunity to formulate a plan and begin to gather all the ingredients you would need to improve the taste?

Here is the challenge for today. When given the lemons of life, understand the choice is up to you. You determine how and what you make of the lemons. You can either focus on their bitterness and do nothing, or you can begin to make lemonade and turn the sour into sweet.

*Difficult situations don't make you; they reveal
who you really are.*

• *Rose Russell*

Who's There?

We are all familiar with the feeling of taking one step forward only to find ourselves knocked back two steps at a moment's notice. I guess that is just a part of life, a series of successes and regressions, and setbacks.

Here is the question for today. How are you handling your regressions and setbacks? Are you blaming others for what you lack? Do you refuse to accept accountability or responsibility for the choices made? Are you taking the opportunity to learn the lessons taught? Know this, the reversals in our lives are not meant to do us harm, but to equip us for our journey toward progress.

The challenge for today is to find and learn the lessons in both the setbacks and successes. In the words of a dear friend, one thing for sure and two for certain, there is always joy to be found in the journey.

Be thankful for the mistakes they will teach you valuable lessons.

• *Author Unknown*

Organization of Me

I hate to admit it, but I come from a family of planners. If you ask my sisters, they will say that planning is one of the things we have in common. And if you ask them which of our parents this trait is from, without a doubt and unanimously, we will say Mom.

When I was younger, I did not see the value in planning or having a checklist. However, as I have gotten older, I have come to realize there is value in planning. One of the most quoted verses in the Bible is Jeremiah 29:11. This verse serves as a reminder of God's plan for us. If He has outlined his plan and promises to us, then why do we neglect to plan for ourselves?

That is the question for today. Why are you neglecting to plan?

Here is the challenge for today. Start small. Take the time to map out what you want to accomplish. Write down the dreams and goals you want to pursue and achieve. Do not let another day pass you by. You are too extraordinary to be extra ordinary.

Success in not only for the elite. Success is there for those who want it, plan for it and take action to achieve it.

• Jim Brown

Seasons

"For everything there is a season, a time for every activity under heaven," Ecclesiastes 3:1. Like the seasons of the year, winter, spring summer and fall, our lives flow in much the same way.

The winters of our lives are spent in reflection and restoration. The arrival of spring brings hope and renewal. As spring turns into summer, what we learned in the winter and grew in the spring is on full display for all to see. As fall approaches, we prepare ourselves for the winter to come, beginning to shed the old and beginning the process anew.

Here are the questions for today. What are you doing during these seasons? What are you doing to prepare?

Here is the challenge for today. No matter which season you find yourself in, be grateful and learn the lessons each season brings. Prepare to share all you have learned.

Don't waste the season of life you are in now because you
want the next one to come.

• Author Unknown

The thought for today is a proclamation which consists of five simple words. These five words could change or even save your life. These five words if spoken loudly enough and often enough will take root in your heart and mind. These words should cause you to walk a little taller and stand a little straighter.

Are you ready?

Here they are: I am more than enough!

That's it. It's as easy as that. No other words or explanation needed. .

Here are the questions for today. To whom have you been comparing yourself? What are you wishing you had?

Here is the challenge for today. There is no need to try to keep up with the Joneses. You are more than enough. You are uniquely and wonderfully made, flaws, perfections, and all. Know. Trust. Believe.

You are more than enough.

Your greatest responsibility is to love yourself and to know you are more than enough.

• *Author Unknown*

Happy Yet?

"Happy to you" has become my great-niece's expression of choice when she is excited. It has even become her expression of choice when she wants to know if you are happy. In short, anyone or anything she is happy to see receives a "happy to you."

Here is the question for today. Have you forgotten what makes you happy? Have you allowed others to dictate your amount and level of happiness?

Here is the challenge for today. When you see something that makes you happy or puts a smile on your face, simply say "happy to me." Go ahead and laugh. But use this as a reminder—a reminder of what brings you joy. I promise after a while your happiness meter will be overflowing.

A glad heart makes a happy face.

• *Proverbs 15:13*

Change of Focus

In the remake of the classic movie Karate Kid, starring Jaden Smith and Jackie Chen, Jackie Chen's character says to Jaden Smith's character, "Your focus needs more focus."

I was thrown off by the comment because in the scene, Jaden Smith's character was in a full martial arts split with sweat pouring down his face. He looked utterly worn out. As the movie continued, I began to understand the comment.

Here is the question for today. What are you focusing on? Are you focused on the negativity around you? Or are you focused on not feeling confident in your skills and what you bring to the table?

The challenge for today is to change your focus. Focus on what you can control. Focus on what makes you unique and special. It is okay that others may not see it. Keep your focus on you, and the rest will fall into place.

Always remember your focus determines your reality.

• George Lucas

Purposefully Designed

As a little girl, I learned a song in Sunday School. It was a simple song that went something like this. "I am a promise. I'm full of possibilities. I am a promise with a capital P. I am a great big bundle of potentiality. I am trying to hear God's voice, and I am trying to make the right choice. I am designed to be anything God wants me to be."

Here is the question for today. Where did you lose your promise? When did you forget you were designed and destined for greatness? Don't you know you are filled with an infinite number of promises, an endless number of possibilities? No matter where you are in life, you have potential for greatness.

Here is the challenge for today. Dust off your promising potential and step into your greatness.

Every great dream begins with a dreamer. Always remember, you have within you the strength, the patience and the passion to reach for the stars and change the world.

• *Harriet Tubman*

Attention, Please

Maya, my great-niece, and I were having a conversation. I'm not sure if you have ever had the pleasure of having a conversation with a two-year-old, but the conversation consisted of me trying to interpret two-year-old speak. After giving up on trying to translate, Maya speak, I finally resorted to saying, "Oh, really?" and "Is that right?"

I guess Maya could tell I was not invested in the conversation. My lack of interest in the conversation and her frustration with having to repeat herself got to her. She finally threw her hands up, grabbed my face, turned it to hers, and said, "You, pay 'ttention Auntie Joy!"

Well, that certainly caught my attention.

The question for today is this. What do you need to pay more attention to? Is it your mental, spiritual or emotional health?

Here is the challenge for today. Take time for you. Do not allow the stresses and strains of life to cause you to forget about you. In the words of my great-niece, "You, pay 'ttention."

Pay attention to the little things. They're more important than you think.

• Matt Gutirrez

Thirsty

"You never miss your water till your well runs dry" is a saying with which most people are familiar. It is used to explain why loss, such as a break up or loss of a job, was experienced.

Here is the question for today. Have you ever thought maybe the well was never full with what you need in the first place? Ouch! So many times, we find ourselves running, chasing after people or things we believe will quench our thirst. We believe these things will fill the dry, barren lands which exist in our lives.

Here is the challenge for today. Check your water source. If your source has left you thirsty, dehydrated, or dried out, it may be time to tap into a new source. The truth is water is never meant to leave you high and dry but renewed and refreshed.

*A drop of water is worth more than a sack of
gold to a thirsty man.*

· *Author Unknown*

Perfect Practice

My dad is the king of seeing the bright side of a negative situation. In fact, he has several sayings the family has affectionately dubbed Sheppard-isms. One Sheppard-ism my sisters and I heard from Dad was "You practice like you play."

Here is the reason. Practice is where you work out the kinks and mistakes. It is where you fine-tune your craft, so on the day of the big game or performance you can go out and have fun. There's no need to worry, because muscle memory will take over.

Here is the question for today. Why do we slack when it comes to practice then expect to produce and perform flawlessly when the pressure is on?

Here is the challenge for today. Instead of dressing for the part you want, practice in the role you have. Perfect your craft, so when the time comes to perform, you are more than ready, equipped, and able.

It is better to be prepared for an opportunity and not have one than to have an opportunity and not be prepared.

• *Whitney M. Young*

Bend Not Break

The late, great Whitney Houston sings one of my favorite songs. In this song, she freely admits her struggles and the obstacles she encountered. Aww, but the best part of the song is when she sings about how she picked herself up and declared with head held high "She was not built to break." And would you like to know why? Why was she able to say with all certainty she was not built to break? It is because while she was in the struggle, she found herself. She found out she was more then she thought she was.

Here is the question for today. Whom do you need to tell or remind you are not built to break? No matter what life throws at me, I will not break. Oh, I may fall, sure enough, but I am getting back up again.

This is the challenge for today. Get back up. Do not stay down there, wherever your "there" might be. Do you know why? It is for no other reason than this; you are stronger than you give yourself credit for being. You were not built to break.

Life doesn't get easier or more forgiving, we get stronger and more resilient.

• Steve Maraboli

Is This Me?

Most of us have children in our lives, either our own, our family members or those we have picked up along the way. That means an awful lot of folks have either watched or are familiar with the Disney classic, Mulan.

On the surface, Mulan is a typical Disney story about the bad guy wanting to take over the world and the good guy coming in to save the day. However, if you look a little closer, you will see the story of acceptance. Specifically, Mulan's acceptance of herself. In the movie, she asks, "When will my reflection show who I am inside?"

Here is the question for today. Do you believe in yourself? If not, what is stopping you from doing so?

The challenge for today is this. Cheer for yourself. Sometimes, you must recognize and know self-validation is needed and is better than any validation man can ever give. So, go ahead, show who you really are inside.

Become so confident in you who you are that no one's opinion, rejection or behavior can rock who you are.

• *Author Unknown*

Will You Go?

I have a confession to make. I am a little embarrassed to admit it, but here goes. Deep breath... Hi, my name is Joy, and I like to watch nature shows. (Insert laughter here).

I was watching a nature show recently in which the filmmakers were following a mother cougar out hunting for food to feed her and her three cubs. Her first few hunts were unsuccessful. After the failure of her last hunt, the mother cougar had a choice to make. Should she stay in familiar hunting territory or leave her cubs behind and travel into Unknown territory miles away to find the food needed to feed her family?

The question for today is this. How determined are you? Are you willing to leave behind the known and venture into Unknown territory to bring life-giving food to those around you?

Here is the challenge for today. Understand and know determination and faith go hand in hand. Step out confidently on faith, determined your hunt will be successful.

Take the first step you don't have to see the whole staircase, just the first step.

• *Dr. Martin Luther King Jr.*

Freedom

Freedom is a double-edged sword. On the one hand, it is a privilege taken for granted by many. On the other hand, it is a privilege unattainable and withheld from those deemed less than worthy by some to receive. It is important to remember the gift of freedom in all forms is not something simply given; it is earned and comes with a price to maintain.

Here is the question for today. How much is your freedom worth to you? Please understand I am referring not only to physical freedom, but also mental freedom and emotional freedom; freedom from those things that keep you bound, render you immobile, stagnant, and filled with doubt.

Here is the challenge for today. Face your fears, and fight to remain free. You have worked too hard and come too far to fail to reach for the prize of freedom and not to claim what is rightfully yours.

*You can't separate peace from freedom because
no one can be at peace until he has freedom.*

• Malcolm X

Don't Think, Know

"Who does she think she is?" This is a phrase most have heard or even said out of frustration or, dare I say, even jealousy towards another. However, what happens when the frustration is turned inward and becomes self-destructive, self-sabotaging behavior?

Here is the question for today. Why? Is it because we have allowed the opinions and expectations of others to dictate or define who we are? Are we believing we belong in the "boxes" into which people place us?

Here is the challenge for today. Break out of the box. Take the limitations off the way you see yourself. There is more to you than even you can see. Let today be the day you no longer ask, "Who does she think she is?" Instead, say, "I know who I am, and I am ready for more."

*Don't be confused between what people say you
are and who you know you are.*

• Oprah Winfrey

Lost and Found

"Where have you been?" It is a question we have either been asked or have asked a time or two. Usually, when you hear this question, regardless of your age, gender or relationship status, it signals trouble is on the horizon.

Here is the question for today. Have you ever stopped and asked yourself, "Where have I been?" Where was I when I lost my peace? Where was I when I lost my joy? Where was I when I lost my faith?

Here is the challenge for today. This challenge requires action. Are you ready? Retrace your steps. Make your way back to the lost and found. Retrieve what was lost. Retrieve what belongs to you. In short, go get your stuff, because all missing things deserve to be found.

Sometimes the things you lost can be found again in unexpected places.

• Daniel Handler

Remove the Plastic

Growing up, we all had that one relative or friend who had a room, or rooms, in their home filled with furniture covered in plastic. Go ahead and laugh. But you know the type of furniture you were unable to look at, breath on, or touch. As a child, I never understood the purpose of having a living room you were unable to live in.

Here is the question for today. Which gifts or talents are you covering up? What purpose are you refusing to walk or live in because you're waiting for a particular person or occasion to arrive?

Here is the challenge for today. Take the plastic off. Take the plastic off your gifts and take the ropes down blocking access to your gifts- your purpose. You were not created to be selfish but to share. Invite others to share in who you are. You never know, if you make it comfortable enough, they just may just sit down and stay for a while.

Use your talents they are precious gifts given to you to put to work.

• Robyn O'Brien

Time for Cake

Have you ever baked a real cake? Not a boxed cake, but one from scratch? Did the recipe have more than four steps?

When my sisters and I were younger, Mom often baked cakes from scratch. When the time came to place the cake into the oven, she would say, "Do not jump. Do not move. Leave the cake alone." The reason for her warning was simple. The more you move, check on or touch the cake before it's fully cooked, chances are the cake will fall, rendering it inedible.

Here is the question for today. Have you ever been faced with a cake situation? Have you ever been faced with a situation where the more you jumped and moved, the longer it took for things, including you, to settle?

Here is the challenge for today. Stop moving around and checking things. Leave the cake alone. The more you worry and open the oven door, the more you delay the baking process which results in a loss of peace, clarity, and understanding.

*Learn to calm down the winds of your mind,
and you will enjoy inner peace.*

• Remez Sasson

In the Middle

As a kid, did you ever play monkey in the middle or keep away? If you have never played, here is how it works. One person stands in between two people. And just as the title says, the people on either side do their best to keep an item away from the person in the middle. The person in the middle runs back and forth between the two, trying to get the item. The game ends when the person the middle either gives up out of frustration or obtains the coveted prize they were after.

Here is the question for today. How often have you found yourself running or wavering between two decisions? How often have you found yourself wondering if you should stay in that relationship or stay at that job? After becoming exhausted from the back and forth, did you simply give up without making a decision?

Here is the challenge for today. When you find yourself in these moments, stop and ask: What am I chasing after? When I catch it, is it going to be what I want? Is it going to bring me happiness? If you can say yes to any of these questions, then continue. If not, then it may be time to end the game.

May your choices reflect your hopes, not your fears.

· *Nelson Mandela*

Run

In high school, my sister was on the track team, where she ran the anchor leg on the 4X100 relay team. There was one race in particular we still talk about to this day. This particular race was the race to determine whether the team would qualify for the state track meet.

The race began ordinarily enough when the first runner had the team in contention. Unfortunately, by the time the next two runners finished, the team was in last place. They were so far behind the team should have given up. However, when my sister got the baton, she ran like her life depended on it—catching and passing each runner in front of her, not stopping until she reached the finish line.

The question for today is this. What are you allowing in your life to hold you back? What do you need to run towards as if your life depends on it?

Here is the challenge for today. No matter what the condition the "baton" is in when it's passed to you, take it. Run with it. Know your purpose is to do better than those before you. Like my sister did, run with a focus unmatched. Block out the naysayers and doubters because you are already better than you were yesterday.

*Challenges make you discover things about yourself
that you never really knew.*

· *Cicely Tyson*

Ugly Mess

Are you familiar with the story of the ugly duckling? It is a story of a duck who was made fun of for not looking like everyone else. However, what the other ducks thought was ugly was a different type of beauty.

Here is the question for today. How often have you been unable to see your beauty? Know you are too beautiful to sit in and accept the ugly mess of others, the ugly mess of criticism, the ugly mess of what society deems as beauty, the ugly mess of trying to fit into someone else's definition of beauty.

Here is the challenge for today. Stop what you are doing. Look in the mirror and say, "The creator fearfully and wonderfully made me. There is no one else like me. Can't no one do me better than me."

Beauty begins the moment you decide to be yourself.

• Coco Chanel

Go Get It

Are you familiar with the story of the Little Engine that could? The Little Engine that could was told he could not be a train due to his size. He was laughed at by much larger trains. That was until he was the only one who was able to make it up a steep hill when the more massive, more experienced trains failed. Why, you may be wondering? I am so glad you asked. The answer is simple. It is the action for today, Go Get It. By repeating the mantra, "I think I can" to show his belief in himself, he did." He succeeded because he didn't doubt that he could,

Here are the questions for today. Why do we allow others to dictate who and what we are to be? Why do we let others discount our talents, gifts, and purpose, due to their inability to see how fabulous we are?

Here is the challenge for today. Be your own cheerleader. When the crowd is silent, be like the little engine that could and say to yourself, "I know I can." Regardless of the obstacles, setbacks, or setups, I'm going to keep pushing forward. Make today the day you go get what is yours.

The moment you want to quit is the moment when you need to keep pushing.

• *Author Unknown*

Simon Says

Have you ever played the game Simon says? If you have, then you know the premise of the game is to test your ability to listen and follow the instructions given. Sounds easy, but here is the question.

What happens when you unknowingly become Simon? That was the lesson I learned the other day. I was talking on the phone, looked over, and saw my two-year-old great-niece mimicking every move, word, and gesture I made. For that moment, I was her Simon.

The challenge for today is to be mindful of how you carry yourself. Be mindful of the words you say, gestures you make, even the relationships you are in. The truth is that someone is always watching you, Simon.

Integrity is doing the right thing even when no one is watching.

• C.S Lewis

Vision

While I was out shopping with a friend, she mentioned she had forgotten her glasses and was unable to read the label on the item in her hand. Being a good friend and master problem solver, I handed her my glasses. She put them up to her eyes, took one look at me, and said, "I still can't read it. In fact, these didn't help at all, they gave me a headache."

The question for today is this. What is your vision? How many times have you forced your ideas and dreams on someone, due to perceived potential or because it is right for you, it must be right for others, too?

Here is the challenge for today. Stop. It is that simple. The beauty of individuality is that we all see in different ways. This is what I learned from my friend. Your vision belongs to you, and mine belongs to me.

It's not what the vision is, it's what the vison does.

• Peter Senge

Mad for What?

"Whatcha mad at?" is the question I ask my five-year-old great-nephew when he becomes so frustrated words seem to escape him. The question is designed to provide him an opportunity to breathe, become calm, and find the words to articulate his anger. What I find most interesting is that when he finally can articulate his rage, he is not angered by another person or situation; he is angry with himself.

Here is the question for today. Have you ever been angry, not at a situation, but at yourself for allowing someone or something to take you out of your character?

Here is the challenge for today. When you begin to feel yourself stepping away from who you are, simply ask yourself, "Whatca mad at?" Often, we hold onto and carry disappointment, resentment, and anger that was never ours to begin with. Release it. You will be much better for it.

*Holding onto anger is like drinking poison and
expecting the other person to die.*

• *Author Unknown*

Left for Dead

How many times have you stepped on a scale and said, "Whew, I have a few extra pounds to get rid of?" As I was saying this to myself for possibly the tenth time in one day, the realization struck me. I was not carrying a few extra pounds. I was carrying around dead weight. Ouch.

Here is the question for today. What weight are you carrying that is dead? It could be a dead relationship or a dead-end job. Whatever it is, the longer you hold on to what should be buried, the longer you remain weighed down.

Here is the challenge today. Begin to shed the extra weight. You may have to start small, with baby steps, but it can be done. Remember that there is a reason dead things are buried. The longer they stay above ground, the more likely they are to begin to stink.

*Be strong enough to let go and wise enough to wait
for what you deserve.*

• *Author Unknown*

Handle Your Truth

From the movie *A Few Good Men,* "You can't handle the truth" is one of the most recognizable lines in modern movie history. This historic scene takes place in a court room, where Lt. Daniel Kaffee, played by Tom Cruise, is questioning, or should I say bombarding, Col. Nathan R. Jessep, played by Jack Nicholson, with question after question, searching for the truth. No longer able to keep his composure, Jessep, pushed to the breaking point, responds in frustration with the now famous line.

Here is the question for today. What is a truth you refuse to accept about yourself? What reality are you refusing to accept because that would mean exposing the ugly parts of who you are? Some things we want to remain hidden, even from ourselves.

The challenge for today is to embrace, then face, the truth. Finally, after embracing and facing reality, begin to conquer your truth, no longer letting it define who you are. Instead, take the lessons learned and allow them to refine you. You can handle the truth.

You can't talk about truth unless you talk about yourself.

• *Cornel West*

Little Red Hen

Are you all familiar with the story of the little red hen? If not, here is a quick summary. The little red hen had a group of friends she asked to help her work her wheat farm, pick the wheat, grind the grain into flour, turn the meal into bread dough and finally help her place the dough in the oven. The reward would be eating the bread together. At each step in the process, the friends said no until the finished product was produced.

Here is the question for today. How many of us have bandwagon friends? Such friends only want to enjoy the outcome of our hard work and dedication but are unwilling to walk with us through the process.

The challenge for today is two parts. First, reevaluate your friend list. Second, reevaluate the type of friend you are. In the end, the little red hen's friends proved to be there only to reap the benefits of her work, so she dealt with them accordingly. Are you a bandwagon friend or a help with the work type friend? The choice is up to you.

In life we never lose friends, we only learn who the true ones are.

• Author Unknown

Burned Bridge?

Do not burn bridges is a universal life lesson we are all taught. However, somewhere along the way, we have experienced a burning bridge. We've either burned a bridge or had a bridge burned. Regardless of which side of the bridge you were on, the result was the same. The bridge that connected you to a person, place, or thing is now no longer in existence. So often, depending on the circumstances, we wonder why and how the disconnection took place.

The questions for today is this. What would cause someone to sever the connection?

The challenge for today is to stop questioning if the decision was made to burn the bridge. Let it be. Sometimes in our want and need to be connected, we rebuild the bridge, only to experience the burn once again. If the bridge is out, the connection is lost. That's okay. Some bridges are not meant to be rebuilt.

> Sometimes burning bridges isn't a bad thing... it prevents you from going back to a place you never should have been to begin with.
>
> • Author Unknown

Beautiful Reflection

"Mirror, mirror on the wall, who is the fairest of them all?" Have you ever looked at yourself in the mirror and thought, I am super cute today? I know I have, especially when I have my favorite outfit on or my hair freshly done. But did you know you are beautiful each and every day. Even on your worst days, you are still beautiful.

Here is the question for today, why do we focus on outward beauty only? Discounting the impact inward beauty has on how we see ourselves.

Here is the challenge for today, understand and accept beauty is not just outward, but inward as well. So, queens, fix your crown and say "Mirror, mirror on the wall, I know I am the greatest of them all."

Beauty comes from within, a beautiful heart creates a beautiful person.

• *Kenyan Proverb*

Love

There was a popular song sung by Tina Turner many years ago entitled "What's love got to do with it?" I like to think when she was singing these words and asking this one important question, she was speaking from experience. At one point, she proclaims from the depths of her soul that love is nothing but a second-hand emotion.

I beg to differ. Love is not a second-hand emotion. It is one of the primary feelings, if not the primary feeling, that drives us all.

The question for today is this. Do you love the right things?

The challenge for today is to do a love check. Are you serving others because of love? Maybe it's because of the need to be seen. Are you supporting others because of love or for the chance to have a front-row seat at their demise? What's love got to do with it? Love has everything to do with it. Let today be the day you check your level of love.

Love makes your soul crawl out of its hiding place.

• *Zora Neal Hurston*

Living Single, Martin, Friends, and *The Golden Girls* all have one thing in common. Can you guess what it is? The answer is friendship.

The question for today is this. What kind of friend are you? Are you one who surrounds yourself with people exactly like you? Do you have a Maxine Shaw in your life, that one friend who is raw, unfiltered, with a tough exterior but soft on the inside? Or do you have a friend like Phoebe, who is a bit scattered but makes the most sense? Do you have a friend like Pam James who is ready to jump into action at the drop of hat and ask questions later about why she needed to jump?

The challenge for today is this. Embrace the friends who are not like you. The beauty in accepting people for who they are is valuing the different perspectives they bring to your life.

Friendship is the hardest thing in the world to explain. It's not something you learn in school. But if you haven't learned the meaning of friendship, you really haven't learned anything.

• *Muhammad Ali*

What You Eat

"You are what you eat" is a saying familiar to us all. This phrase typically refers to what we eat physically. But how about the other areas in our lives?

Here is the question for today. What do you eat? Is it a daily dose of positivity or negativity? Is it a daily dose of love or hatred? Is it a daily dose of self-doubt or regret?

Here is the challenge for today. Watch what you eat. If you consume doubt, replace it with confidence. If you take in hatred, replace it with love. If you chew on regret, replace it with joy. If after reevaluating what you have been feasting on physically, mentally, and emotionally is weakening you instead of strengthening you, perhaps it is time to change your diet.

Tell me what you eat and I will tell you what you are.

• French Proverb

Heart's Desire

At first glance the story of Pinocchio is a cautionary tale told to children about the pitfalls of lying- not being truthful. While that may be, you need to look a bit closer. This story is also about the desires of the heart. Let me explain. Pinocchio, a puppet, desired to be a real boy. His father Geppetto desired a son, a companion he could call his own.

The question for today is this. What is your heart's desire? What I find interesting in this story is the way Pinocchio and Geppetto set out to obtain what they desired. Pinocchio lied, stole, cheated, and sought outside resources, which were unable to help him, and ultimately led him further away from his intended goal. Geppetto, on the other hand, kept his desire to himself and still did not end up with what he wanted until he shared his wish with the one who was able to help.

The challenge for today is to know it's okay to have desires, but know you cannot reach them alone. Share them with others and watch all the wishes you make upon stars come true.

Delight yourself in the Lord and he will give you the desires of your heart.

• *Psalms 37:4*

Sister's Keeper

There is a phrase we have heard and have most likely have used ourselves when describing our friendships. The phrase is "I am my sister's keeper." From time to time we need to check our "sister" status. It may sound funny, but it's the truth. So often we claim sisterhood; however, our words and actions say otherwise.

Here is today's question. Are you really a sister or an imposter? Are you keeping secrets shared in confidence, or are you sharing secrets with others the first chance you get? Are you sharing in her joy or harboring resentment at her success?

The challenge for today is to keep your sister in all things by becoming a "safe" to hold secrets, an accountability partner when needed, and the leader of her cheering section when she succeeds. In short, keep your sister as you want to be kept, and watch her do the same for you.

There is strength in sisterhood.

• Author Unknown

Stop Thief

If you lived in the Sheppard household, were a friend of one the Sheppard girls, or hung around our dad long enough, you might have heard the following Sheppard-ism. "Don't let little people steal your joy." I will admit that I often found myself growing tired of hearing my dad say this. If I am honest, there were times when I was younger that I did not understand fully what he was saying. That was until I experienced the theft of my joy.

In that moment the following question came to me. Have you thought so little of your talents, your abilities, and your dreams that you are stealing your own joy by believing what others have said about you?

Here is the challenge for today. Think big. Stop shortchanging yourself. Accept that you deserve joy, happiness, and peace. Make today the day you stop stealing from yourself.

Never let anyone steal your happiness, it's not theirs to take.

• Author Unknown

Step Out

No man left behind. The captain goes down with the ship. I am my sister's keeper. I am a ride or die person. No matter how you say it or the moral code you chose to live by, what connects theses mantras is simple. It is the principle of sacrifice.

The questions for today are this. Who are you willing to step out of your lane or comfort zone for to bring back in line? Are you prepared to utilize resources at your disposal to assist a friend or stranger?

Here is the challenge for today. Look for opportunities, real opportunities, to step out of your lane to bring a friend, a loved one or even a stranger back in line. Understand that stepping out of line will cause you temporary discomfort; however, your sacrifice of comfort will undoubtedly bring comfort to someone else.

Often stepping out of your comfort zone is not careless irresponsibility, but a necessary act of obedience.

• Andy Stanley

Yes and No

We have all been overcommitted, saying yes to accommodate others while wondering how in the world can we can make something happen. As much as I would like to be two people, I am not.

The word for today is to let your yes be yes and your no be no. The over-commitment of our time, energy, and efforts is a sign to others that we are not to be trusted. Saying no is okay.

Here is the question for today. How often do you over commit yourself out of fear or in order to be accepted?

The challenge for today is this. Establish boundaries and stick to them. Disappointing someone in the short term is far better than a relationship lost for a lifetime. Yes or no. Make a choice and stand behind it.

The oldest, shortest words- "yes" and "no" are those which require the most thought.

• *Pythagoras*

Fat, Lady, Who?

"It ain't over 'til the fat lady sings" is a familiar phrase.

The question is this. Who is the fat lady and what song is she singing?

The challenge for today is to write, sing, and produce your song. You are uniquely and wonderfully made. From the color of your eyes, the texture of your hair, and yes, dare I say the color of your skin, you are equipped with a song only you can sing. A song shared with others will bring healing, hope, love, forgiveness, and peace.

Sing your song. Do not worry if you sing a bit off-key. Melodies and tempos are meant to change as that is what makes your song special. I do not know who the fat lady is, but I know my song's not over, and she cannot sing my song better than I can. Are you ready to sing?

No Matter what people think of you, always keep singing your own song

· Author Unknown

Comfort

Being the wonderful auntie that I am, I volunteered to watch my niece for my sister and brother-in-law. At the time she was four years old. When I walked into the house, I was greeted at the door with a laugh and good luck from my brother in law as he and my nephew left the house. My niece was watching one of her favorite movies, *Zootopia*. I knew instantly why he laughed.

Here is the question for today. Have you ever been asked to step out of your comfort zone? For most, being uncomfortable requires a level of courage and willingness for a time period to live in the discomfort. It also opens the door for others to experience our vulnerability along with us. As I watched my niece dance around the room, comfortable in her skin, not caring who saw her, I realized she did not care if I joined in or not, she just wanted me to put in the effort.

That is the challenge for today. Put in the effort. Get out of your own way and experience new things. Once I realized that was all I needed to do, I did it. What a lesson to learn.

It's ok to be scared. Being scared means you're about to do something really, really brave.

· Author Unknown

No More Tears

Weeping may endure for the night, but joy comes in the morning. We have all been there mourning the loss of something or someone we just knew we could not live without, only to find the longer we spent throwing a party of pity, where the gifts we opened consisted of loneliness, self-doubt, bitterness, anger (the list could go on and on), we were delaying our joy.

The question for today is this. What are you mourning that is keeping you from your morning joy?

The challenge for today is to stop accepting gifts that cause you to mourn. Your morning time is here. Weeping has taken place far too long. You have endured enough; it is time to celebrate. Congratulations, ladies and gentlemen, you have made it to the morning's joy. Let the celebration begin.

The more you praise and celebrate your life, the more there is in life to celebrate.

• Oprah Winfrey

Clap Your Hands

"If you're happy and you know it clap your hands" is a song we learn as children. The instructions given in the song are to clap only if we are happy. Unfortunately, along the way to adulthood, we learn to clap even when we are sad. In short, we learn to clap with whatever emotion we were feeling.

The question for today is why? Often, as natural peacemakers not wanting to rock the boat, we feel the need to nurture, provide, and protect those we love, but at what cost to ourselves? What price to your health? What cost to friendships? What cost to relationships? The list could go on and on.

The challenge for today is self-care. Take a few minutes each day to reconnect with yourself. Discover what recharges your batteries. There is nothing wrong with being selfish on your behalf. So if you're happy and you know it, clap your hands.

Happiness is an inside job. Don't assign anyone else that much power over your life.

• *Mandy Hale*

Inside Voice

Have you ever been told to use your inside voice? But what is an inside voice? Is it the voice used when physically indoors? Or is it the voice used internally that others are unable to hear, the one we use to work out our thoughts and feelings internally?

The question is not about our voices, but the messages we speak inwardly to ourselves, the messages we believe to be true.

The challenge for today is to change the channel. If your voice is on the station of negativity, change the station. If your voice is on the station of self-doubt, change the station. If your voice is on the station of loneliness, change the station. If your voice is on the station of bent up, broke up and jacked up, change the station. Remember this, your inside voice mirrors your outward projections. Are you ready to change the station?

Talk to yourself like you would someone you love.

• Brene' Brown

You vs. You

A wise woman, my mom, when offering advice on addressing conflicts or concerns which involved others would say, "You address the issues and never attack the person." That is the secret to fighting fair. Thank you, Mom, for the advice.

Here is a question. What if the person you need to fight is you? Have you ever had to fight; I mean really fight with yourself? Let us be honest. Not all fights are fair, and not all fights are products of our unhappiness. Sometimes, we are just in a fight.

Here is the challenge for today. When fighting yourself, address the issues. Confront them head-on. Do not skirt around or sweep them under the rug. Some issues we face are purposely designed to build our faith and promote growth. Some fights are designed to increase our head, heart, and hand strength. Are you determined enough to stay in the fight and say, "I won't, and I can't let go, I have too much riding on the outcome!" So, who is ready to fight?

Challenges are what makes life interesting; overcoming them is what makes life meaningful.

• *Joshua J. Marine*

Elephant

The word for today is a serious one. There are two things you will need to do before you answer, that is, if you are up to the task. The first is think about your response, and the second is to be honest with yourself.

This question is for you alone to answer. Ready? Here goes, "Are you the elephant in the room?" Now that you have stopped laughing. Think for a moment. Are you the one who upon entering a room instantly changes the atmosphere? Whether for good or bad, the energy of the room shifts. We are designed to be change agents. When we enter a room, our presence, our character, and integrity should speak on our behalf before we ever utter a word.

The challenge for today is to check your elephant status. Is your energy drawing or repelling people? Are you someone people are clamoring to know, or are they running to hide from you? Only you can determine the type of elephant you are when you are in the room. So, what kind of elephant will you be when you enter the room?

Energy is contagious positive and negative alike. I will forever be mindful of what and who I allow into my space.

• Author Unknown

Stay

How many times have you been in the middle of a conversation, listening to a person speak, when the realization hits that you have checked out of the conversation? We have all been there. We have all checked out of a conversation because of the person presenting the information, the length of time they have been speaking, or, let us be honest, lack of interest in the conversation. Here is the problem with "checking out." Vital information is missed.

The question for today is "Do you hear what I hear?" Remaining in the conversation is difficult and at times even painful, but stay in the conversation.

The challenge for today is your continued commitment to stay present and in the moment. Hang in there, regardless of the direction the conversation may take, for when you stay focused and present, you are less likely to miss your blessing.

If we miss the moment, we miss the clues. In the present we, when we allow ourselves to be fully live there, we are restored, made wiser, made deeper and happier.

• Marianne Williamson

Truth or Dare

The game Truth or Dare is designed for a person to blindly chose a dare or share a fact about themselves before knowing the question that will be asked. This game is usually not played very long. Here's the reason. The purpose of the game is to make players uncomfortable. Truth or dare tests players' ability to be truthful with themselves and others, as well as their strength, nerve, and overall resolve.

So, here is the question. How many times have you played truth or dare when it came to making a crucial decision regarding a relationship, job opportunity, finances, etc.

The challenge for today is to determine the price you are willing to pay. Understand that there will be a cost for speaking and living your truth. There is a cost for stepping out of your comfort zone, leaving negative thoughts and people behind. Only you can determine the price you are willing to pay. Truth or Dare?

May your choices reflect your hopes, not your fears.

· *Nelson Mandela*

Sacrifice

If you have had the pleasure of watching the Disney movie *Frozen*, you no doubt are familiar with sisters Elsa and Anna. At the start of the movie we learn Elsa has the magical power of making snow and ice appear out of thin air. Unfortunately, with the untimely death of their parents, Elsa goes into hiding, no longer spending time playing with Anna.

Elsa began to live in self-imposed isolation. Anna, on the other hand, still wanting to have a relationship with her sister, asks Elsa one question. The question is simply, "Do you wanna build a snowman?" That may seem like an odd question, but for Elsa it became a painful one. The word for today is sacrifice. For Elsa, the question was a reminder of what she chose to give up.

The question for today is this. What are you willing or needing to give up to reach a goal or fulfill a dream?

The challenge for today is to understand that not all sacrifices are bad. Yes, you may be without for a while, having to endure the pain of the loss. But just like Elsa, when what you sacrificed returns, you will be better than ever. So, who's ready to build a snowman?

Believe in something even if it means sacrificing everything.

• Colin Kapernick

Restoration

The word of the day is restoration. If you have ever watched a home improvement show, you know that once a home is found the potential buyer or contractor walks through it to determine if it will be worth the time, effort, and energy the restoration process will take. Once the walkthrough is complete, someone will ask: "What do you think?" If they feel the project is worth the time, their response is usually, "It has good bones." As the person watching the show, we may say no way or go with what is new. We may wonder why waste the time or resources. However, when the finished product is revealed, we ooh and ahh along with everyone else.

The question for today is, who or what in your life has "good bones?" Who needs the attention, time, energy and resources only you possess and can give to restore its beauty?

The challenge for today is to look around you and see who has bones which need restored. Please understand, I did not say former beauty. For when the restoration process is complete, the finished product will be even better than before.

And he will give you beauty for ashes.

• Isaiah 61:3

Direction

We have all been unsure of where we were going or where we are supposed to be. We either became lost due to missing information when the directions were given to us or lost by our own doing, because we just knew where we were going. However, it turned out we were wrong.

Here is the question for today. How did you become lost? Where did you lose your way? We all give and receive instructions in different ways. Some will draw a map, others will write them out, and some will do both. However, even with directions, we still manage at times to get lost.

The challenge for today is to trust the reroute, for in the reroute, you may discover something beautiful just off the beaten path.

> Sometimes the creator will put a road block in
> your path to redirect you.
>
> • Iyanla Vanzant

Bear the Wait

You most likely have heard or even said, "He'll never put more on you than you can bear." The question is, can you bear the wait? How many times have you taken on extra, thinking He was not moving fast enough? But you needed an answer, a resolution right away, a resolution that you thought would bring you peace. Did you know by taking matters into our own hands, we add extra pounds and steps to the process?

The question for today is what do you have to lose by waiting? Seriously, take a few moments and think about what you have to lose by waiting. Will you lose time invested in a job that no longer fulfills you? Are you in a relationship where you are no longer valued or are taken for granted? Will you lose the agony of waiting for a promise to be fulfilled? Waiting is hard and we often want to rush the process.

The challenge for today is wait. Yes, the waiting process is difficult and not easy to understand. I beg you to take your hands off whatever "it" is and trust the process you are going through. Keep in mind that when you rush the process, you're adding both weight and wait.

Don't go back to less because you are too impatient to wait for the best.

• Author Unknown

Overflow

Many of us have at one time or another been late to an event and had to sit in the overflow area instead of in the main arena. For many the idea of sitting in the overflow causes issues or problems. The overflow represents being late or the possibility of missing out on a first-hand experience.

Here is the question for today. Why? Why are we so afraid of the overflow? Why do we feel the need to be in the middle of the action? Here is the beauty in the overflow. While you may not be in the main arena, you are still in the building.

The challenge for today is to remember you are in the building. You may not be in the front right now, but you are in the building. Use this time to grow, develop, and learn all you can. Perfect your vision, your mission, your craft, and your purpose for when it is your time to move from the overflow to center stage. Your overflow experience can be used to encourage someone else. So, get ready to overflow.

You are a continuous work in progress and your happiness will eventually overflow into the lives of those around you.

• *Zelna Lauwrens*

Not Broken

We have all gone through something we thought would break us. A relationship we thought would last forever ended. A seemingly healthy child became sick without warning. Our dream job suddenly ended. A loved one passed away. While going through these experiences and possibly unbearable grief and guilt, you may have thought you would surely die.

Here is the question for today. Did you ever think instead of death these experiences were refining you, pressing and shaping into a beautiful diamond?

The challenge for today is to remember life happens. I know the shaping and pressing process is not easy and does not feel the best. In fact, it could be harder to understand and accept than the loss experience. In those times when you are unable to understand, the who and the why, remember simply you are a diamond with fractures and flaws and a story only you can tell. Your fractures and flaws add character to your story. In no way are you broken. So, shine.

Life tried to crush her, but only succeeded in creating a diamond.

• John Mark Greene

Remember

The classic Disney movie *The Lion King* tells the story of Simba. After the tragic death of his father Mufasa, Simba forgets who he is. Have you ever been at a place in your life you never thought you would be? Have you ever been on the outside of your dreams, looking back and wondering how in the world you got there? "Where did I lose my way?" you ask. "Where did I lose me?" Much like Simba, regardless of opportunities given and support received, still, you did not know who you were.

The question for today is, how? How do I make my way back to where I lost me?

The challenge for today is stop and reconnect with what makes you you. You are never too old to remember who you are. Much like Simba remembered he was the son of Mufasa. There is power in knowing who and whose you are.

Once you know who you are you don't have to worry anymore.

• *Nikki Giovanni*

Faith over Fear

A few years ago, I took a trip with a good friend to Las Vegas. Before our trip we planned out where we would go and which activities we would do. On our to-do list was to zipline down Freemont Street. What very few people know is that I am afraid of heights. The top of a step ladder is too high for me.

While we were walking up the stairs to reach the platform where we would be harnessed in and given our final instructions, the thought came to me that fear cannot live where faith resides. I know you may be thinking being on solid ground, as opposed to 76 feet in the air, would have been a better place for my life changing epiphany. I absolutely agree, but you never know when or where life lessons will occur.

Here is the question for today. Have you ever been afraid over a situation in your life? Have you ever be fearful of making a wrong decision? As I stood on the edge of the platform, just before it gave way, I questioned why I thought this was a good idea.

The challenge for today is to have faith in yourself. Believe you have made the best decision for you. No second-guessing. Leave no room for doubt. Faith and fear cannot occupy the same space. Once I let go of my fear, I was able to enjoy the ride.

When fear knocks on your door, send faith to answer.

· Author Unknown

Silence

Several years ago, a dear friend came to me and disclosed she had been diagnosed with a rare form of breast cancer. As she was telling her story, I was at a loss for words. This was a road I had not personally traveled and was unsure of how to respond. It was at that moment I made a choice not to speak, but instead to simply hug my friend.

The question for today is how often have you tried with words to fix a situation? How often have you been offered unsolicited advice by someone trying to be helpful? The moment I decided not to speak or try to fix her situation, I learned the power of compassion, sympathy, and silence.

That is the challenge for today. Offer a reassuring touch or a listening ear accompanied by a closed mouth. Sometimes people just want to know you're there, present and in the moment offering a safe space or a refuge where they can just be. The power of touch and silence can speak louder than words ever could.

Silence is a source of great strength.

• *Lao Tzu*

Break Habits

Experts say it takes 30 days to form a habit. That means, good or bad, in 30 days, 720 hours or 43,200 minutes, habits are created. Patterns are funny things. Once formed, they are tough to break.

Here is the question for today. Have you ever found yourself responding to situations, only out of habit? Do you give a routine response without listening to what was being asked or said? Are you functioning on autopilot?

Here is the challenge for today. Begin to move and respond with purpose, no longer out of habit but with a plan. Begin to pay attention to your surroundings and those who you allow in your inner circle. Understand this; habits that make you better are worth keeping, but some need to be broken immediately. Begin today to check, reevaluate, release, and refine your habits. It just might save your life.

Your small daily habits and behaviors determine the overall trajectory of your life.

· Author Unknown

Love's Foundation

"Love is patient; love is kind. It does not envy; it is not rude. It is not self-seeking. It is not easily angered; it keeps no record of wrongs. Love does not delight in evil but rejoices with truth. It always protects, always trust, always hopes always perseveres. Love never fails" (1Coronthians 13:4-8a NIV).

This familiar verse is often recited at weddings as a reminder to the bride and groom of the constant need for love to remain present throughout the marriage. But what about before the wedding and the joining of the two lives together?

Here is the question for today. When you are in a season of singleness, do you take the time to show yourself patience and kindness? Are you keeping a mental record of your shortcomings, causing self-doubt, destroying your self-worth?

The challenge for today is to extend trust, perseverance, and protection to yourself. Let today be the day you vow from this moment forward that no one will or can outdo the compassion, trust, honesty, and love you have for yourself.

You, yourself, as much as anybody in the entire universe, deserves your love and affection

• Author Unknown

Hold This

Hi, my name is Joy and I am guilty. I am guilty of telling myself I am only running into the store (insert your favorite store name here) for one thing. I do not need a cart. Go ahead and laugh because we all know what is next. Yep, you guessed it; I not only pick up the one thing I went into the store for but a few others, as well. It's not that I did not stick to my budget or plan to purchase only one thing, but I tricked myself into believing I did not need help. I did not need to grab the cart as I walked into the store.

Here is the question for today. Why do we refuse help when it is offered? How difficult is it really to allow others to help share, hold, and carry what is in our heart and on our mind?

Here is the challenge for today. Check on your friends, family and those close to you. If you see their arms are full, do not just let them struggle and bear the weight alone. But instead, grab their arms and help balance the load. They may not let go of what they are holding, which is ok—just be there, hold them up not just with words, but also with your actions. We all need a helping hand now and then, so put your hands up.

A kind gesture can reach a wound only compassion can heal.

• *Author Unknown*

Labor of Love

When I had my first child at 20 years old, I had no idea how painful childbirth would be. No amount of reading, watching videos, or speaking with women who had already gone through the process could prepare me for the pain I would experience.

Here is the question for today. Which labor pains are you experiencing? Are you experiencing pain associated with loss? Maybe your pain is associated with a renewed purpose, a vision, mission, or promise given only to you.

No matter the stage of labor you find yourself in, here is the challenge for today; trust the process. Trust that your instincts will not fail during the birthing process. Oh, you may need to call a timeout to regroup and gather your strength. You may become frustrated, angry at everyone along the way. You may even want to place a few people in a headlock if they get too close. Just hang in there; do not cut the process short. Here's why. The blessing as it grows, much like a child, will far exceed the pain experienced during the birthing process. Who is ready to push?

Now Jabez was more honorable then his brothers and his mother called his name Jabez, saying because I bore him in pain.
• *I Chronicles 4:9*

Beautiful Creations

I am a huge fan of nature shows. One evening I was watching an episode that focused on unusual looking animal species. As I watched the show, I found myself saying, "Beauty is more than skin deep." While some of the animals did not exhibit features we would consider beautiful, that is precisely what made them attractive. It was their uniqueness and acceptance thereof.

This is the question for today. What do you need to accept about yourself that you find not so beautiful? Which flaws have you yet to embrace?

The challenge for today is to begin to see your beauty. Accept those things that make you who you are. You are fearfully and wonderfully made. Your beauty is not just skin deep; your beauty is found in your thoughts, your character, your integrity, and your conversation. Let today be the day you let your beauty shine through.

The kind of beauty I want most it the hard-to-get kind that comes from within: Strength, Courage, Dignity.
• *Ruby Dee*

Posture Correction

In the movie *A Knight's Tale*, William Thatcher, played by the late actor Heath Ledger, was on a quest to prove his worth to others. Have you ever felt the need to prove yourself to others, wondering why they are unable to see how fabulous you are?

Here is the question for today. Have you ever thought about why you believe the validation of others somehow makes you worthy, even to yourself?

The challenge for today is stop, look, and listen. Stop doubting your worth. Change your focus from where you are to what you have overcome to get where you are. Finally, listen to who you are. A turning point in the movie came when William's lineage was read aloud. Sometimes, you need to hear who you are. Know you come from a line of strong, resilient people who have overcome. These people, like you, may have fallen but got back up again. Your people have greatness and gratefulness running through their veins.

I am Joy, daughter of Rochelle. Rochelle is the daughter of Vivian. Vivian is the daughter of Laura. Laura is the daughter of Ellen. Ellen is the daughter of Hannah. Knowing this, I cannot help but stand a little taller.

When our hearts turn to our ancestors, something changes inside of us. We feel a part of something greater than ourselves.
• Russell M. Nelson

Your Story

By a show of hands, how many remember when choose your adventure books were popular? If you did not have the pleasure of growing up during the height of their popularity, let me explain how the books worked. The author wrote an adventure story, and just when you got to the good part, the cliffhanger or where the characters were faced with making a crucial decision, the story abruptly ended. The reader was then given two options to move the story forward. Looking back, that was a lot of pressure to put on an eight-year-old.

Here is the question for today. Why are you allowing others to write your story? Why do they write the narrative to your life, choosing which path is best for you?

Here is the challenge for today. Choose your own adventures. Make your own decisions. Write your own narrative. We may not all have had the same opportunities, but we all have one critical thing in common. We all have the power of choice. You have the choice to write and live your narrative and speak your truth. Here's the best part. Much like the choose your own adventure books, if you're not happy with the current story, you have the time to write a new one.

You either walk inside your story and own it, or you stand outside your story and hustle for your worthiness.

• Brene Brown

All Aboard

"This train is gone." was and still is my mom's way of letting my sisters and me know she was ready to leave wherever we were. Over time and after having been left a few times, we learned when mom said, "This train is gone." she was serious. We'd better quickly wrap up whatever we were doing and get to the car before she did or we'd would get left. Oh, and did I mention, she was not coming back to get us? What I learned was the value of time, not only my mom's time but my time, as well.

Here is the question for today. What or whom do you need to tell this train is gone? How much more time will you spend waiting for things to change? How long will you remain in a holding pattern standing at the train station platform, waiting for the train of time to return?

Here is the challenge for today. When the conductor yells, "All aboard, this train is gone!" that is your cue to move. Don't look back. Don't wonder if you made the right decision. It's time to move. There's no need to remain stagnant in a place of indecision. It's time to move. Don't stay frustrated at those who were unable to honor your time. It's time to move. Are you ready to leave the station? Toot! Toot! All aboard. This train is gone.

Don't say, "there is still time." or "Maybe next time." Because there is also the concept of "it's too late.
• Author Unknown

Narrative

"If you can't say anything nice, then don't say anything at all." This is a saying most people are familiar with. This pearl of wisdom is often told to us as children as a way to teach us not to speak negatively or disparagingly about others.

Here is the question for today. If we are given this nugget of wisdom as children, then why do we not apply the same advice when we speak of and to ourselves? One of the most difficult things to do is to recognize our own value and accomplishments and share those things with others.

Here is the challenge for today. Do not downplay your achievements and success. Begin to rewrite your narrative. Take a minute; look at yourself in the mirror and begin to speak. Name and accept all the wonderful things that make up who you are. Remember there is death and life in the power of your words. How can you speak life if you are dead on the inside?

Take care how you speak to yourself, because you are listening.
· *Author Unknown*

Are You Blind?

What do the movies *The Hunch Back of Notre Dame* and *Finding Nemo* have in common? Take away the obvious that they are good movies and each of the main characters faced some level of adversity. I'll give you a hint; think about each of their physical appearances. They each would not have been considered beautiful by society's standards. Let me give you another hint. They each had friends and family who were able to look past their outward appearance to see the beauty within.

Here is the question for today. Why do we focus on a person's outer packaging instead of what is on the inside? How often have you passed on an opportunity to befriend someone simply because they did not look like you?

Here is the challenge for today. Take a moment to evaluate the blind spots in your life. What is holding you back from accepting and meeting others where they are? Recognize the blind spots, then begin to do the work to eliminate them. In the words of Michael Jackson, "I'm starting with the man in the mirror."

People judge by outward appearance, but the Lord looks at a person's thoughts and intentions.

• I Samuel 16:7

What's Missing?

Have you ever tried to make a cake or fix your favorite meal without having all the ingredients needed? When this happens, you usually have two choices. You can make do without the ingredients, improvise and hope for the best. Or you can stop what you're doing, go out and purchase what is missing. If you chose to do without and improvise, the end product on the outside may look complete. However, taste is another story.

Here is the question for today. If knowing missing ingredients will effect the taste, then why continue with the cooking process? Is it because you hope the outward presentation of the dish will cover what is lacking in taste?

Here is the challenge for today. Take a few moments and evaluate what in your life is missing. Find out what is keeping you from feeling completely whole? On the outside, you appear put together; however, inside is a different story. Are you missing love? Are you missing peace? Are you missing self-acceptance? Whatever you are missing, begin to find and incorporate the missing ingredients into your life. Keep this in mind, half of a person was not designed to live a whole life.

God can restore what is broken and change it into something amazing.

• *Joel 2:25*

Whole

When celebrities announce the birth of their newborn child, the recent trend is for them to post a picture of the newborn's foot, leg, or arm - any part other than the child's face. For many, just a glimpse of the child is enough to make them happy.

Here is the question for today. If you are satisfied with just a glimpse, a piece of, imagine what would or could happen if you were given complete access?

Here is the challenge for today. Why are you settling? Why are you satisfied with a piece, when you deserve the whole? A glimpse is meant to bring happiness for a moment, but the presence or a better look will sustain and keep you for much longer.

Settling for less than the best is a key characteristic of a person, who doesn't feel that they are worthy of more.
• Crystal McDowell

Helping Hand

There is a Chinese proverb known by many the world over that says. "Give a man a fish and you feed him for a day. Teach a man to fish and you feed him for a lifetime." This proverb is usually quoted or referenced when discussing the value of hard work or the need not to give someone a handout.

Here is the question for today. What if the person just needs you to extend your hand or believe in them? They have the education, drive, passion. They have all the potential in the world; they just need one person to say, I see you and I will help you.

Here is the challenge for today. Consider who needs your help? Who can you partner with and say, "Today, not only will I give you a fish, I will teach you to fish and provide you with the proper lure to catch more?" Sometimes it's more than teaching and hoping the student gets the lesson. Give the lesson, reach out your hand and watch your legacy flourish.

Service to others is the rent you pay for your room here on earth.
• Muhammad Ali

Speak Out

We have all been there. We have all either apologized for something we did not do or for expressing our feelings that caused discomfort to others. I was having a conversation with a friend recently and found myself apologizing after every uncomfortable 'feeling" comment. Finally, my friend stopped talking, looked at me, and said, "Stop saying you are sorry. Stop apologizing for how you feel." Needless to say, that hit me like a ton of bricks.

Here are the questions for today. Why are you apologizing? What are you saying sorry for? Who is the apology to? Often times, we do not want to upset the status quo but choose rather to be seen and not heard. But is that fair? No.

The challenge for today is own what you feel. It is not your job to make others feel comfortable while diminishing or placing yourself on the back burner. Discomfort is ok; it is a part of life. Start today to speak up, speak out, and own your truth. In the words of a well-known reality star "I said what I said." Own how you feel.

Never apologize for how you feel. No one can control how they feel. The sun doesn't apologize for being the sun. The rain doesn't say sorry for falling. Feelings just are.
• Author Unknown

Broken Blessings

There is a song written and sung Matt Redman featuring Tasha Cobbs Leonard entitled "Gracefully Broken". When I first read the title of the song, I thought immediately, clearly, he has never broken a bone. There is nothing graceful about broken bones. The truth is that being broken is painful. In short, he did not put a lot of thought into the title.

However, after reading the song lyrics, I began to understand. There is more to being broken than wearing a cast. The breaking process involves separation from what it holds fast to.

Here is the question for today. What do you need to break free from? Who do you need to tell no more?

The challenge for today is experience the break. Do not place a bandage over the broken area. Yes, the healing process will be painful; however, the blessing is in the brokenness. Once you are healed, you will be stronger and better than ever.

Broken things can become blessed things, if you let God do the mending.

• Author Unknown

Thrive

When my younger sister was in the third grade, she brought home a tree sapling from school and gave it to our mom for Arbor Day. My sister was so proud of her gift; she asked if she could plant it in the yard. Dad, on the other hand, less impressed, found the perfect spot to plant the sapling - right between two large, relatively mature trees.

Go ahead and say it, poor little seedling. It had a good run from the schoolhouse to the backyard. But that is not the end of the story. That sapling, despite a rocky start, has thrived. In fact, some forty plus years later, it has outgrown, outlived, and outlasted, the two trees it was planted between.

Here is the question for today. What do you need to fight to overcome? Who do you need to show that your strength can surpass their expectations of you?

Here is the challenge for today. Do not give up. Press on. Hold on. Hang on. Be like the tree in my parents' backyard. Refuse to die. You may be run over by the " lawnmower" of life. You may be mistreated, discounted, and denied. However, continue to fight. In the end, when those who counted you for dead see how you have not only survived but also thrived, they will only be able to wonder how.

I shall not die, but live, to declare the works of the Lord.
· Psalms 118:17

Hold On

"I regret to inform you…" "We have decided to go in a different direction." "Thank you for your interest in…"

We have all been on the other end of disappointing news. News that was an outcome we did not expect or want. Over time, a steady stream of disappointments can cause you to lose faith in yourself and in your ability to bounce back.

Here is the question for today. How are you handling these setbacks? Are you setting up camp in the swamp of sadness, living in a state of regret?

Here is the challenge for today. Know you are more than enough. Disappointments and setbacks happen. Even our best thought out, laid out plans do not always go as expected. In those times remember and know that you are more than enough. Greater is coming. Hang in there.

The size of your success is measured by the strength of your desire, the size of your dream, and how you handle disappointments along the way
• Robert Klyoski

Amendments

As children, we are taught rules and regulations designed to keep us safe. Rules such as looking both ways before crossing the street or saying please and thank you make life better.

But what happens when the very rules designed to keep us safe no longer do so? I'm not speaking of society's rules but about the standards or moral code you have chosen to live by. What happens when those standards or rules become outdated?

Do you continue to follow them as they are or add amendments? Those are the questions for today.

Here is the challenge for today. Take the time to reassess and amend, if necessary, the personal rules, regulations or moral code you live by. Just because it has always been done does not mean it's the best or right way to continue. Do not be afraid; not all change is bad. Some changes may just save your life.

> Change is sometimes needed to better yourself, love yourself and truly be happy. Never stop working on the best you can be. It's a life long endeavor.
>
> • Angelique LaForest Trembly

The Present

Have you ever bumped into someone you have not seen in a long time? The first words spoken usually are "Oh, I remember you." Or, "I remember when you used to…" At this point in the conversation, you are wracking your brain to figure out where you know this person from, what do they remember and how quickly can you escape the conversation.

Here is the question for today. Why do we instantly worry about what will be said? Is it because we may know the person from a time in our lives we would rather forget?

Here's the challenge for today. Take back your power. "I knew you when" and "I remember you" are phrases designed to keep you bound to the mistakes and poor decisions of your past. They are not designed to speak to who you are now. Know this, you remain bound to your past when you refuse to live in your present.

I owe no explanations for my flaws. I don't have to justify my mistakes, my past, or my insecurities. I am growing and learning. Let Me Live.

• *Mama Zara*

Sanctuary

As far back as the middle ages up to the present day, those who were facing persecution and needed to find a place of safety would run, not walk, to the nearest house of worship and claim sanctuary. Here, the priest, bishop, pastor, etc. provided protection. If they stayed within the walls of the church or city, they were safe. No one, not even the law, could touch them. But what happens when the very place of safety ceases to be safe?

Here is the question for today. When have you stopped being a safe place for people in need to run to? When did you lose the capacity to hold your brothers' or sisters' hurts and fears in secret because you were too focused on your own?

The challenge for today is to return to being a sanctuary. Return to being a place of safety for those in need, a place of love, a place of healing for the wounded and broken. In short, return to being a place hope, a sanctuary.

The word of the Lord is a strong tower the righteous run into it and are safe.

• Proverbs 18:10

By Invitation Only

When my sister and brother-in-law married some nineteen years ago, it was comparable to any celebrity wedding. Because my sister was the first sibling to get married, my mother was adamant about two things. First, it was an adult-only wedding reception. Second, if guests did not RSVP for the reception, they would have to wait in the designated holding area and be seated after those who sent their RSVPs. To ensure this took place, guests had to check-in upon arrival at the reception before the hostess escorted them to their assigned tables.

Here is the question for today. How often do we allow uninvited guests into our lives? This could be in the form of taking on problems that are not ours or allowing boundaries we have set for ourselves to be violated.

Here is the challenge for today. Check the invitation. Not everything or everyone deserves entrance into your heart, mind, spirit, body, or soul. Remember extra baggage is just that – baggage.

Sometimes you have to protect yourself at all cost.
· *Floyd Mayweather Jr.*

Listen

"A closed mouth don't get fed" is a saying some may or may not be familiar with. This saying refers to a person not speaking up to express a feeling, want, or need.

But here is the question for today. What happens when you open your mouth too much, not taking the time to listen to the thoughts and feelings of others? What happens when, due to your need to be heard, the words you speak no longer hold weight? Instead, your words become noise to the listener's ear.

Here is the challenge for today. Before speaking, take the time to listen. Listen to the words being spoken. Listen not with a response or rebuttal in mind. Listen with an open mind and a watchful eye. Here's the reason. If you open your mouth to speak too soon, you could be helping someone to plan and execute your downfall.

Sometimes the best thing you can do is keep your mouth shut and your eyes open. The truth always comes out in the end.

• Author Unknown

Weakest Link?

Over the years, I have read my fair share of books on how to lead, how to lead authentically, and how to develop leadership presence. I have even attended numerous conferences and workshops on the subject, with the hopes of learning the how-to of becoming a great leader.

In all of the many books I've read, conferences I've attended, and self-guided courses I've taken, one of the common themes discussed was the team being only as strong as the weakest link. Usually, at this point, the author of the book or workshop presenter provided a series of tips and tricks to boost the strengths of the other team members in order to hide the weakness of one.

Here is the question for today. What happens if you are the link determined to be weak? Are you truly weak or are you not being utilized properly?

Here is the challenge for today. Do not mistake the idea of weakness for others' lack of understanding what you bring to the table. We are each equipped with gifts and talents which, when allowed to develop and utilized correctly, add to the strength of the chain. You are not the weak link in the chain. Your strength just has not been tapped into yet.

Every weakness contains within itself a strength.
• Shusaku Endo

Taste Buds

Have you ever wanted something so badly you could taste it? I mean, it's so close not only for you to smell, but you can pick out and isolate each ingredient, from the salt and pepper, all the way to the vanilla extract.

Here is the question for today. Just because you can taste it, does it mean it's the right thing for you? Oh, don't get me wrong, the smell is wonderful, the packaging is beautiful; however, the question remains, is it right for you?

Here is the challenge for today. Take a moment to reevaluate if what you want, what you have set your mouth to taste will remain right even after you get it. It's ok if your taste buds have changed; that just means you have left more for someone else, and a cleaner and clearer pallet for yourself.

Oh taste and see that the Lord is good, blessed is the man who trusts in Him

• *Psalms 34:8*

Own It

There is a saying that goes, "What happens in Vegas stays in Vegas." It usually refers to the possibility of questionable activities that took place while in Vegas.

Here is the question for today. What happens when your Vegas "actions" are no longer hidden but on full display for all to see? Will you be ashamed, continually looking over your shoulder, waiting for the other shoe to drop? Or will you be standing tall without a care in the world?

Here is the challenge for today. We all have had our fair share of "Vegas" experiences. If your actions or words have wronged or harmed another, knowing or unknowingly, do not sweep it under the rug. Go make it right. Only by making it right, owning your actions and words, will you find peace of mind. As a good friend's favorite song asks, will you have the ability to Live Your Best Life?

Living your best life is your most important journey in life.
• Author Unknown

Mine

When my daughter was younger, one of her favorite shows was *Dora the Explorer*. If you are familiar with the show, you undoubtedly know the cast of characters, from Dora all the way down to Swiper. Did you ever notice when Swiper approached, trying to take from Dora something important that she needed to complete her mission, she faced Swiper head-on, looked him in the eyes, stood firm with conviction and authority and told him NO. She did not do this one time; she continued until he got the message and gave up.

Here is the question for today. What in your life do you need to "Swiper"? Is it your peace of mind? Your health? Your finances? The list could go on and on.

The challenge for today is when you feel Swiper approaching, look him in the eye, and with head held high and shoulders back, declare to Swiper "No Swiping. You do not have permission any longer to take what is mine."

There is power in the word NO.
• Author Unknown

Clean Up

I cannot be the only person who does not get out the car right away as I arrive home. It was at one of these times while I was sitting in my car that I noticed a stray cat walk across my driveway, root around in my freshly laid mulch, and proceed to poop. Yes, I said poop. I could not believe it. When he finished, he politely covered it up and walked away. I was so upset! How dare this cat I don't know walk into my yard, do his business and leave. Now I'm left to clean up his mess, mess I did not ask for or want.

That's when it hit me. Here is the question of today. How often have I acted like that cat by walking uninvited into a situation, depositing my two cents, then leaving the mess for others to clean up? Or have I allowed the messy opinions, thoughts, and assumptions left by uninvited cats to change my fragrance, the core of who I am?

Here is the challenge for today. Before making a deposit, make sure what you have to offer is wanted and/or needed. If left untreated, mess has a way of festering, growing, and attracting resentment. On the off chance that you have left a few unwanted deposits behind, take the opportunity to make things right.

A sincere apology has three parts: I am sorry It is my fault What can I do to make it right?

Life Lesson

I have a dear friend who suffers from a disease that causes her to live with constant body pain. One day while we were talking on the phone, she mentioned she was not doing well. She was experiencing an unbearably higher than normal pain-filled day. I, being who I am, thinking I was showing empathy and compassion, made the following statement, "I hope you feel better soon."

Well, that was the wrong thing to say, because before I knew it, my friend proceeded to tell me off. I don't remember all that was said, but what I do know is she caught me off guard and then hung up after she said her piece. Needless to say, I was in my feelings. How dare she hang up on me? Who does she think she is? Before I could call her back, it hit me. Joy, you don't listen. She's asked you repeatedly not to say feel better soon.

Here is the question for today. How often, out of our selfish need to make sense of discomfort, do we contribute to an already pain-filled situation?

Here is the challenge for today. Recognize it's okay to live with the brokenness. There are feelings, emotions, and situations that cannot be fixed with words or empty gestures of empathy. Pain is a part of the life story we all must feel. Thank you, my friend. Message and lesson received.

*How we walk with the broken speaks louder than
how we sit with the great.*

· Bill Bennot

Faith's Escape

What happens when you place eight beautiful, smart, college-educated, multiple degree holding, professional women with various personalities (mostly Type A) in a room and give them forty-five minutes to solve a mystery to escape? The answer -CHAOS. This is what happened when a group of friends and I decided an escape room outing would be fun.

I learned a few things that day. First, Type A personalities do not work well together. Second, escape rooms with more than four people are not fun. Third, and most importantly, leaders have the hardest time following because they are unable to control where they are going. Ouch!

The question for today is why is it difficult to follow? The answer is simple. It requires faith to follow.

Here is the challenge for today. Exercise your faith. Be willing to accept that you do not have all the answers. Taking a step back and learning from others is okay. That is what faith is all about. Finally, we know that faith does not make things easy. Rather, it makes things possible (Luke 1:37). If we had exercised a bit of faith in each other we would have solved the mystery with time to spare.

*Faith is taking the first step even when you
don't see the whole staircase.*

• *Martin Luther King, Jr.*

Sunflowers

Sunflowers have an interesting story. When they are young, they follow the path of the sun. When the sun can no longer be seen, they turn and face each other to gather energy and strength because they have not yet learned to harness and store the sun's energy for cloudy days.

Here is the question for today. How much more could we accomplish if we, like the young sunflowers, in our times of lack, uncertainty, or weakness, turn toward each other instead of away from each other isolating ourselves?

Here is the challenge for today. Know you are not alone. Lean on and depend on your source of spiritual strength, friends, and family, who have proven themselves to be true. Share their energy and strength. Allow them to hold you up in your time of need, until you can harness the power of the sun, once again.

Never be ashamed about being broken, because strength is nothing but pain that's been repaired.

• *Trent Shelton*

When I began my year of yes, I did not set out to write a book. My goal was to encourage family and a few friends. I did not know how my saying yes would start me on my own self-discovery journey. While on this journey, I have received encouragement, support, and love from so many. I would be remiss if I did not take the time to say thank you.

I first must give honor where it is due to my parents, Theodis and Rochelle Sheppard. I will never be able to thank you enough for teaching me the power of prayer, love, faith, and family. To my sisters, Lisa, Keziah, and Thea, what can I say? I have the best sisters in the world. Thank you for allowing me to share our journey as sisters throughout the pages of this book. Cameron, Mckenna, and Tracy II, my three heartbeats, what an honor it is to be your mom. It has not always been easy, but I thank you for your understanding, patience, and love. I am incredibly proud of each of you. Thank you for inviting me along your life's journey.

There is a special group of people I must say thank you to also as they were the first to begin the journey. Along with my family, they embraced my year of yes challenge and allowed me to share many of the thoughts found in this book. Thank you Lisa, Myra, Jai, Janel, Anish, Andrea B., Andrea F., Cynthia, Stephanie, Shawn, Mykka, Brittany, Janeen, Cat, Abria, Angelia, Carla, Dezerae, Yolanda, Valerie, Sylvia, Margaret, Layah, Lenore and Abria. A special thank you to my First Lady Jeana. And an even bigger thank you to one of my best friends, Veralyn, who had she not recommended I read the Year of Yes, by Shonda Rimes, none of this would be possible.

I would also like to say thank you to my Grovehurst Consulting and Not Really Random Family. Sarah Strobel and Crystal Springer thank you for the work you have done on this project; you are amazingly invaluable. Lisa Sheppard Floyd – thank you for believing enough in my words to take a chance on an Unknown author and publish Joy for the Journey. It means more than words can ever say.

As I bring this to a close, thank you to my nieces (Acacia, Maya, Taylor, and Alli), nephews (Christopher II, Malcolm, and Tyrell) and Christopher I, the best brother-in-law ever, for allowing me to tell your stories as well. Pat, thank you for letting me use your home as my "office." If I have forgotten to mention anyone, please charge it to my head and not to my heart. I love you and appreciate you all.

About the Author

Tamura J. Gadson graduated from Walsh University with a B.A. in Organizational Development and Leadership. She has held several leadership positions related to people development, mentoring and coaching. Gadson began encouraging others with Joyful Moments, a recurring newsletter piece. This was the first time she shared her writing with others.

In 2019, a friend recommended that Gadson read the book Year of Yes: How to Dance It Out, Stand In the Sun and Be Your Own Person by Shonda Rhimes. After reading Gadson was inspired and challenged herself to commit to writing every day for a full year. Gadson fulfilled her challenge by texting encouraging words to family and friends. It was this idea and its positive reception that led Gadson to publish her first book, Joy for the Journey. Joy for the Journey combines two of Gadson's great passions: motivating and encouraging others.

Gadson lives in Akron, Ohio and is the mother of three. She is currently pursuing a Master's Degree in Adult and Continuing Education from Rutgers University.